ATHLETICS: THROWING

Also in the Pelham Pictorial Sports Instruction Series

Chester Barnes: Table Tennis
Henry Cooper: Boxing
John Dawes: Rugby Union
Bob Wilson: Soccer
Richard Hawkey: Squash Rackets
Rachael Heyhoe: Women's Hockey
Barry Richards: Cricket
Ken Adwick: Golf
Paul and Sue Whetnall: Badminton
Jack Karnehm: Understanding Billiards and Snooker

In preparation

Denis Watts: Jumping and Vaulting
Celia Brackenridge: Women's Lacrosse
Brian Jacks: Judo
David Haller: Swimming
W. G. Scull: Gliding and Soaring

Pelham Pictorial Sports Instruction Series

Howard Payne,
assisted by
Rosemary Payne

ATHLETICS: THROWING

Photography by Howard Payne

Pelham **Books**

First published in Great Britain by
PELHAM BOOKS LTD
52 Bedford Square
London WC1B 3EF
1976

ISBN 0 7207 0925 3

Filmset and printed in Great Britain by
BAS Printers Limited, Wallop, Hampshire

Contents

Introduction

In the English-speaking world the throws in athletics have long taken a back seat to the more popular running events, and, at various times, they have been called the 'Cinderella events', 'the poor relations of athletics' and even 'the events which always let the country down in points-scoring matches'. There are several reasons for this: for example, the throws are more technical and difficult to learn than the other events; they require special, sometimes expensive implements, concrete circles and safety nets; competitions are more difficult to organise; and, unless the spectators are well informed, the throws don't offer the immediate and obvious excitement of a race. In the newer developing countries, such as many of those in Africa, athletics is still a young sport and the throwing events are taking a long time to get established. But even if we take the example of Britain, with its excellent athletics organisation, we see that although we have produced the occasional outstanding thrower, like shot-putter Arthur Rowe for instance, we have had an army of runners — Roger Bannister, Derek Ibbotson, Robbie Brightwell, Dave Bedford, Brendan Foster, Dorothy Hyman, Lillian Board and Andrea Lynch among them — who have been the world's best, and we have relied too much on them in international matches. Because of this, the Press and the public have tended to ignore our less successful throwers, and the attitude has filtered all the way down to the grass roots of athletics where youngsters have been discouraged from taking up the field events. Then, of course, British facilities for the throws have never been adequate, and we have been able to produce only a very few expert coaches in these events. This situation has existed throughout the Commonwealth and even to a certain extent in the U.S.A. in some events.

Fortunately, however, this situation has begun to change in recent years, and we have seen the start of a great upsurge in popularity of the throws. On television, instead of having to watch every lap of the 10,000 metres, we are being shown recorded highlights, followed by slow-motion replays, of the field events, and with skilful presentation these can be exciting and informative. With the advent of the league system in athletics, clubs are now becoming aware of the need to encourage their throwers. We may have a long way to go before we have the highly organised systems for bringing throwers to their full potential that exists in such countries as East Germany and Finland, but a start has been made and the British throwers are gaining respect from their opponents in other countries. This new attitude has already been reflected in improved performances in the schools, and each season sees 'unbeatable' records being smashed.

This is all as it should be, for the throws can be very satisfying events to watch and to compete in. Just a little more knowledge of them than for the running events is needed by both spectators and competitors. We hope in this book to provide that knowledge so that you can enjoy the thrills of the throws as much as we do !

The Competitive Throwing Events

The International Amateur Athletic Federation rules provide for four men's events in the throws — the shot, the discus, the javelin and the hammer. All, except the hammer, are also thrown by the ladies. There are no physiological reasons to prevent a woman throwing the hammer, and presumably there has never been any demand to include this event in today's already crowded programmes. The techniques, specifications and rules vary enormously from event to event, and this is how it should be, for it means that no one athlete can specialise in all the events, and many are encouraged to participate. Because of the great differences we'll be looking at each event separately, but some aspects are common to all the throws and these will be mentioned now.

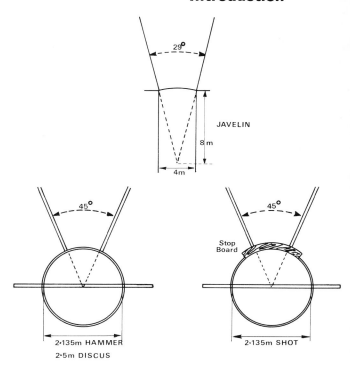

The Throwing Areas

1. The specifications for throwing areas : the drawings (not to scale) show the measurements that concern the throwers. The metal-rimmed concrete circles have surfaces 2cm below the surrounding ground, and all lines are marked with paint or tape. To be valid, throws must land between the sector lines

The shot, discus and hammer are each thrown from a circle into a specified area, which is a 45° sector of a much bigger circle with the same centre, while the javelin is thrown from a runway into a sector of about 30°. The competitor is not allowed to touch the ground outside the circle or runway until the implement has landed, and then he, or she, must leave

Athletics: Throwing

from the rear half of the circle, or, in the case of the javelin, without crossing the scratch line. Usually each competitor is allowed three throws, and the best eight are then allowed three more. Each competitor is credited with the best of all his, or her, throws. If there is a large number of competitors, as for example in the Olympic Games, a preliminary qualifying competition, with just three throws each, is held. A standard is set, and all who throw beyond this standard go into the competition proper, without this counting towards the final result. If fewer than twelve qualify, then the top twelve are taken through to the final, irrespective of distance thrown.

Each throw is measured in a straight line from the front of the circle (or scratch line, in the case of the javelin) to the nearest point of landing of the implement (in the case of the javelin, this must be made by the point, and in the case of the hammer, by the head, the wire and handle marks being ignored). Various methods of measuring are used — by the usual measuring tape, by a special tape from a special datum arc in the landing area, or by the sophisticated optical instrument seen at Olympic Games.

A very important rule governing safety is that during practice implements must be thrown only from the circle or scratch line, and must be returned during either practice or competition by hand — *not* thrown back to the starting area.

Safety
The throwing implements are potentially dangerous objects when treated care-lessly, as is recognised in the rule mentioned in the previous paragraph. Always remember that you, the thrower, are responsible for the safety of everyone around when you release a shot, discus, javelin or hammer. Make sure that no one is within range before you start your throw — if judges or fellow throwers are within range, make sure that they are aware and alert when you throw. Discus and hammer should always be thrown from within a protective wire-netting 'cage', and special precautions are necessary for javelins. Always carry your javelin vertically and never let anyone run in the throwing area — they may run on to the sharp tail of a javelin sticking up from the ground. If you are throwing during a school class pay particular attention to the instructions from your teacher. With proper care there should be no accidents.

Rules and Specifications
The particular rules and specifications relating to each of the throws will be discussed as we come to them — just let it be said that these rules and specifications are laid down to ensure that there is fair play, and that no thrower has an unfair advantage over another, so in competition never use an implement which you know is underweight, or in any other way suspect. If you have your own implements make sure that they are correct by regular weighing and measuring. Some un-scrupulous athletes have used drugs to improve their performances. Besides being against the rules, drugs have been proved to be of doubtful benefit where performance improvement is concerned, and they are medically dangerous.

Never compromise yourself by flouting the rules.

Why Throw?

As a thrower you will often have to face the question which goes something like 'Why do you, an intelligent person, indulge in such an odd occupation as throwing bits of metal around the place?' You may answer seriously that the joy, the pleasure, the frustration and the challenge of throwing can be known only by those who have actually thrown the implements used in athletics. For the few who have that little extra edge in ability there are the obvious rewards of top-class, or even international, competitions with expenses-paid travel to new exciting places, but if these were the only rewards there wouldn't be many throwers around. The British Hammer Circle alone has several hundred members, so hammer throwing must have attractions other than the bright lights of international competition. Unlike the other events in athletics, the throws have the advantage that there is so much room for improvement by the beginner. From first clumsy efforts of a few metres, the enthusiast can steadily improve until he or she has doubled and even trebled the early distances in about two or three years. Thus, if you find satisfaction in the mere learning of a skill, you can have many happy hours ahead with the shot, discus, javelin or hammer. There will be times of frustration when improvement halts, or even reverses, but this only serves to increase your satisfaction later, when with perseverance you again improve.

There is a paradoxical mixture of discipline and freedom in a throw — there must be control of movements in the glide, turns or run-up, but there is always the glorious release at delivery. The psychologists may say that the delivery in a throw is a symbolic throwing away of one's cares and restrictions. Certainly, to feel a fast, well-timed and well-balanced release is to experience the sense of fulfilment felt by the mountaineer when he finally reaches the summit. On occasions we have had a really satisfying throw, and literally jumped with joy! But like all good things the near-perfect throw doesn't happen often, and when it does you worry whether you can do it again, and so you go on — you're hooked!

Although the events are rather arbitrary, invented by man, they are also what we like to call pure in the competitive sense. Barring accidents, you don't have to pound your opponents insensible, kick their shins, 'cut them up' or grind them into the dust — you just have to throw farther than they can. The real pleasure comes from within — when you can throw a little farther than the distance you reached the day before, or perhaps when you reach the same distance with an easier, more relaxed action. As someone who is interested in throwing — you may have started already — you can be assured that training and competition in the athletic throws will enrich your life and give you many hours of healthy enjoyment.

The First Time You Throw

Let's assume that you have decided to have a go at one of the athletic throws. The first thing to do is find an implement and a place where you can throw it. You should approach your school's physical education teacher and seek advice — if you have already left school, your best course of action is to join a club with a throwing area and a good throws coach. Your

Athletics: Throwing

school's physical-education teacher and/ or your club's officials will give you help and advice, but you will find that a lot of initiative will have to come from you, yourself. Not all schools or clubs have a good supply of throwing implements and you may have to beg, borrow or buy your own. Limited grants to buy equipment are available from area associations and national associations so make enquiries before buying expensive implements. Most sports-equipment retailers will have, or can order, throwing implements. You may even get your own made if you have a friend who is a carpenter or an engineer. For instance, training hammers which do not damage the turf can be made from lengths of heavy chain joined loosely together, and attached to a wire and handle.

As a thrower, you will be faced with the big problem that nearly all throwers have to overcome — finding a safe and acceptable place to throw. If you are lucky enough to have an athletic track nearby, you will have to make arrangements with the appropriate authorities so that you can throw at a time when the field is free and you are not likely to be a danger to other users. As a javelin thrower you may have to launch a campaign to have an all-weather javelin run-up laid in your field. If you throw any of the other implements, you may even have to roll up your sleeves, and help mix the concrete for your circles. Lack of facilities never stopped any dedicated thrower!

Learning to Throw
In the throwing events there is always something new to learn, and in this sense you are a learner for as long as you participate in the sport. So you should

2. The coach and the athlete: Dennis Cullum, coach to a number of successful Commonwealth and Olympic hammer throwers, advising Barry Thomas

have a coach — a second pair of eyes to help you when, unknowingly, you begin to deviate from the correct technique. But even more essential is that you should have a coach watching you when you first throw, so that you don't incorporate faulty technique into your method from the start.

Masters' or Veterans' Athletics

This book is really aimed at the beginner in the throwing events of athletics, usually youngsters under the age of about 20, but there is another age category: in recent years many people have taken up the throws for the first time in the over 40s for men and over 30s for women. In America and Canada they call them Masters, in Britain they are Veterans. There are five-year groupings for men: for example, 40 to 44 is the 1A group, 45 to 49 is the 1B group, 50 to 54 is the 2A group, and so on, and at present there are ten-year groupings for women.

The specifications for the Veteran ladies' throwing implements in all age groups are the same as in open athletics. The men in the groups up to 49 years of age throw the same weights as in open competition, but from 50 onwards the specifications begin to change to accommodate the slow decline of strength and speed with age. The exact specifications are in a state of flux, as Veterans' throwing is still a young sport!

If you do qualify by age for Veterans' athletics, and you are an interested beginner, don't rush out and start a strenuous training session. If you haven't done much exercise in the past few years your body won't appreciate a sudden unaccustomed demand on it, so come to physical fitness for throwing gradually. Start with five minutes of gentle jogging and easy stretching exercises each day for a few weeks, and allow yourself six months to a year to regain full fitness for hard throwing.

Note to left-handers
In this book instructions are given for the right-handed thrower. Left-handers will need to make the necessary transpositions.

Note to the ladies
Lady readers please substitute 'she' for 'he' in the technique descriptions.

CHAPTER ONE

Shot Putting

History

Throughout history men have competed against each other in throwing various weights and stones for distance, the Irish and Scots being particularly prone to indulging in this type of amusement. Even today many Scots communities attempt to standardise their annual competitions at 'Highland Gatherings' by keeping certain weights and sacred stones.

Biomechanics research shows that once the weight of an implement is above a certain critical value (and this value depends on the thrower and his strength to a certain extent) the most efficient way of throwing it is to 'put' it — in other words the elbow must be kept behind the hand holding the implement, so that stronger muscles can be brought into action. So it is probable that the early throwers used a technique very similar to today's, which has been further ritualised by the rules.

About the middle of the last century, the spherical cannonball shot was substituted for all the odd shapes and weights which has been thrown, and the weight was standardised at 7·257kg/16lb for men. At about the time of the revival of the Olympic Games in the 1890s the present 2·135m/7ft diameter throwing circle was

introduced, and the rules gradually became more stringent to ensure fair competition. The technique at this time was to hold the shot against the neck, with the body at the rear of the circle, sideways on to the direction of the throw. The right-handed thrower would stand on his right leg and use the free swinging left leg to help the hop, or glide, across the circle, so that he landed with the right leg in the centre of the circle and the left at the front. Without hesitating, he would launch the shot from this position by a vigorous extension of the whole body in the direction of the put.

In the early 1950s, the American Parry O'Brien transformed the technique by starting at the rear of the circle from a position in which the back is turned to the direction of the put, and the shot is carried low and far to the rear in order to increase the time during which the thrower exerts his force on the shot. This, with various minor modifications, has come to be the orthodox style used by most shot-putters today. Several people, including us, had experimented with a rotational method of putting the shot, with foot movements very similar to those used in discus throwing, but had come to the conclusion that although the body moved very fast, the shot tucked into the neck moved no faster across the circle than in the orthodox style. Since then, however, the Russian, Barishnikov, and the American professional, Brian Oldfield, have thrown well over 21·33m/70ft with rotational styles, and caused a controversy like the high-jumping Fosbury Flop *v.* Straddle debate. In this book we will describe both techniques, though placing more emphasis on the simpler orthodox style.

The ladies were slow in coming to shot putting, but then they first took part in the Olympics only as late as 1928. Unfortunately it was mainly over-weight, slow-moving women who first dominated the shot putting scene, and the event gained an undeserved reputation for being unladylike, which it is still struggling to cast off. However, one has only to see the world-record holder, the big, but beautiful Marianne Adam of East Germany, and some of the very feminine pentathletes putting the shot, to realise that the event can be a graceful one, in which a woman loses none of her femininity. It is all a

state of mind anyway, for in places such as Bulgaria and Russia, where strong healthy women are admired, there are great traditions in ladies' shot putting.

Although strength is a factor in shot putting, it should be remembered that the ladies shot is only 4kg/8lb 13oz, and that speed, co-ordination and technique are equally important for achieving big distances. British women's shot putting is definitely lagging behind the rest of the world because of silly outdated attitudes towards femininity, and it is probably the event with the most undeveloped potential. How about it, you interested young ladies?

Specifications
In order that youngsters still growing in strength should not have to struggle with shots too heavy for them, the Athletic Associations have laid down specifications which allow them to develop good techniques and enjoy competition amongst their own age groups. These weights are shown in the table.

Males		
Age group	*Age at 31st August/1st Sept*	*Minimum weight of shot*
A.A.A. Men	19 and over	7·257kg/16lb
A.A.A. Juniors	17 and 18 }	6·25kg/13lb 8oz
E.S.A.A. Seniors	17, 18 and 19 }	
A.A.A. Youths }	15 and 16	5kg/11lb
E.S.A.A. Intermediates }		
A.A.A. Boys }	13 and 14	4kg/8lb 13oz
E.S.A.A. Juniors }		

Females		
W.A.A.A. Seniors } and Intermediates }	15 and over	4kg/8lb 13oz
W.A.A.A. Juniors (E.S.A.A. groups same)	11 to 14 inclusive	3·2kg/7lb 2·6oz

Athletics: Throwing

Key to abbreviations
A.A.A.   Amateur Athletic Association
E.S.A.A.   English Schools' Athletic Association
W.A.A.A.   Women's Amateur Athletic Association

(Note that in international 'Junior' competition, men must be under the age of 20 in the year of the competition and throw the 7·257kg shot, while women must be under the age of 19 and throw the 4kg implement.)

Rules affecting technique

The methods which can be used to throw the shot are very much limited by the rules, the all-important one stating: 'The shot shall be put from the shoulder with one hand only. At the time the competitor takes a stance in the ring to commence a put, the shot shall touch, or be in close proximity to, the chin, and the hand shall not be dropped below this position during the action of putting. The shot must not be brought behind the line of the shoulders.' This effectively bars the thrower from using two hands, or holding the shot at arm's length. The rules do call for the use of a 10cm high wooden 'stopboard' at the front of the circle, and this, when used properly, can be of great help to the thrower, enabling him to remain within the circle after release of the shot.

The Technique—O'Brien Style

Holding the shot
The shot is carried on the base of the fingers, high in the palm, with the fingers spread only just sufficiently behind to prevent it dropping out of the hand. The idea is that you should be able to keep in good contact with the shot, and apply a wrist and finger flick at the last moment.

If you hold the shot in your palm, you won't be able to add this final wrist and finger action, and if you spread your fingers too wide, you will find that you are pushing with only one finger, which can be rather painful!

The stance at the back of the circle
Stand at the back of the circle (farthest away from the stopboard) with your back to the landing area. Grip the shot as above, and tuck it into the neck just to the right of your chin. Raise the elbow away from the body and keep it high and behind the shot throughout the throw—your put will be very ineffective if you allow the elbow to drop and come under the shot as you perform the push with the arm. Move your bodyweight over your right leg.

The glide
The shot is delivered from a position in the front half of the circle, and the idea of the 'glide' is to allow the thrower to move fast and smoothly from the rear of the circle into and through this delivery position. The simplest way to perform this glide is to round and relax the shoulders, crouch over the right leg, without allowing the trunk to bend too much, and use a left-leg kick to initiate a drive across the circle so that the right leg comes down in the

*3. Holding the shot: Russell and Andrew Payne demonstrate
the position of the shot when preparing to throw*

centre and the left reaches the stopboard. The weight remains on the right leg, so the glide is really a very low hop, though coaches avoid the use of this word, because there should not be any up and down movement of the body as it crosses the circle. This almost vertical trunk position produces a simple technique used by many of the world's best putters. Others prefer to use a more difficult start to the glide by going through the so-called 'T-position'. In this, they bend the trunk almost to the horizontal, carrying the shot outside the circle, while at the same time counterbalancing this lean with a horizontal left leg. This refinement of the technique allows the shot to be driven over a slightly longer distance, but it does require good balance and timing, and this takes much practice to perfect.

During the glide across the circle, the shot should rise gradually, and the shoulders should be kept as far round to the starting position as possible, while the lower half of the body begins to turn towards the front of the circle.

4. Shot technique: the sequence shows Geoff Capes, Commonwealth record holder, winning a Europa Cup competition

16

Athletics: Throwing

The delivery

At the end of the glide you should be in a strong throwing position in the front half of the circle. This means that your body-weight will be over a bent right leg in the centre of the circle, shoulders and head still turned to the rear, while your almost straight left leg has come down with the foot against the stopboard, slightly to the left of the line of throw. Without any hesitation, the delivery is started by driving hard with the right leg, so that the right hip is forced to the front, bringing with it the relaxed upper body. The shoulders are swung round, and the right arm (elbow high and behind the shot) strikes a fraction of a second later, and, by the time contact is lost with the shot, the whole body is extended upwards and forwards. There should be no piking at the hips, neither should there be any drooping away to the left. In the delivery some throwers think of an 'up and over' lifting movement, and this is useful if you have a tendency to fall away to the left. All this time your feet should preferably remain in contact with the ground.

The reverse

This refers to the quick change in position of the feet once the shot has been released. The movement causes a reaction which tends to keep the thrower in the circle, preventing a no-throw. The reverse should come fairly naturally, so don't think too much about it or you may start it too soon, before the shot has been released.

The Rotational Method of Shot Putting

The footwork in this method is very similar to that used in discus throwing, except that the feet have to turn much more closely and neatly, because of the smaller circle diameter. Because of the rules, the shot has to be tucked into the neck as in the orthodox style, and only a modified body swing is necessary at the start. Balance is all-important, and any dropping away of the left side in the delivery can be disastrous, if not dangerous because of the presence of the raised-up stopboard. For this reason, it is advisable to throw from a circle without a stopboard during the learning stages. If balance in the turn has been good, the delivery will be much smoother than, but very similar to, that used in the orthodox technique.

Tips for Shot Putting

1   Think of relaxing your upper body all the while, until the final shoulder and arm drive.
2   Orthodox: keep the shoulders as square to the rear as possible, and for as long as possible, during the glide by fixing the eyes on, and pointing the left arm at, a spot about 10m directly to the rear of the circle.
    Rotational: Make sure that the lower half of the body leads the upper part by relaxing the shoulders and thinking of fast feet.
3   As they land, try turning the feet towards the front.
4   Use the left arm for balance, and to start the final movement of the shoulders in the delivery.
5   Keep the left shoulder from dropping in the delivery.
6   Try for full extension at the waist in the delivery.

18

5. *The rotational style: Aleksandr Baryshnikov, c the U.S.S.R., in a display of superb balance an timing in this difficult movemen*

2 3

5 6

8 9

10

11

12

13

14

15

7   Points 5 and 6 may be helped by
    thinking of 'chest up and forwards'.
8   Rhythm is helped by thinking of a
    slow controlled start and a fast finish,

without any hesitation 'for a cup of
tea' in the middle.

9   Keep the technique simple.

CHAPTER TWO

Discus Throwing

History

We have Myron's famous sculpture 'Discobolus' to remind us that discus throwing history goes back to the Ancient Greeks. In those days the discus was made of wood or stone, and was thrown with an underarm action, for accuracy as well as for distance, but there was no standardisation of the specifications or rules. In the nineteenth century the event was revived in two forms — one with the Greek-style underarm throw and the other with a free-style method, and as late as the 1908 Olympic Games there were competitions in both styles. In 1911 the circle diameter was standardised at 2·5m/8ft 2½in. Using the technique of the day — a side-on start and a rotating stepping action into the throwing position—James Duncan of the U.S.A. set a world record of 47·8m/156ft 1in, which stood for 12 years.

Two Americans, Phil Fox and Eric Krenz, in the 1930s pioneered the technique of starting with the back to the direction of the throw, and Bob Fitch, also of the U.S.A., further developed this into the running rotation style common today, and pushed the world record up to 54·92m/180ft 2in in 1946. The world record has climbed inexorably higher and

higher since those days, with many great throwers in turn becoming the holders of the record, but the greatest thrower of modern times is undoubtedly the American Al Oerter, who held the world record for a few years and won the Olympic title no less than four times. Discus throwers, like hammer throwers, seem to stay in the sport for many years, and we have seen men like Adolfo Consolini of Italy, Ludwig Danek of Czechoslovakia, Ricky Bruch of Sweden and Jay Silvester of the U.S.A. dominating the ranking lists for ten years and more.

The ladies were accepted as discus throwers long before they were as shot putters or javelin throwers, and there was a discus event for them at the first ladies' Olympics of 1928. There have been some strong characters in this event — for example Nina Ponomaryeva of the U.S.S.R., who caused an international (athletic) incident when she allegedly shop-lifted a hat in a London store; Tamara Press of the U.S.S.R., who swept all before her; Olga Fikotova of Czechoslovakia, whose romance, and later marriage, with American hammer thrower Hal Connolly, at the 1956 Olympics, caught the imagination of the

Athletics: Throwing

whole athletics world; and Lia Manoliu, now a top official in the Rumanian government. It was Liesel Westerman of West Germany who really showed the event an unladylike aggression, and opened the way for fast and strong throwers such as Faina Melnik of the U.S.S.R., the first thrower, male or female, to throw over 70m/229ft 8 in.

rules do not stipulate the method which must be used for throwing the discus. The technique has developed over the years to take maximum advantage of the circle size. Some throwers have experimented with more rotation and even with a complete extra turn, but there doesn't appear to be any advantage gained over the orthodox one-and-three-quarter turn technique.

Rules Affecting Technique

As in hammer throwing, but unlike in shot putting and javelin throwing, the

Specifications

The weights for the various age groups are as follows:

	Males	
Age group	Age at 31st August/1st Sept.	Minimum weight of discus
A.A.A. Men	19 and over	2kg/4lb 6·5oz
A.A.A. Juniors	17 and 18 }	1·75kg/3lb 13·75oz
E.S.A.A. Seniors	17, 18 and 19 }	
A.A.A. Youths }	15 and 16	1·5kg/3lb 4·75oz
E.S.A.A. Intermediates }		
A.A.A. Boys }	13 and 14	1·25kg/2lb 12oz
E.S.A.A. Juniors }		
	Females	
W.A.A.A. and E.S.A.A.	All age groups	1kg/2lb 3·25oz

(Note that in international 'Junior' competition, men must be under the age of 20 in the year of the competition and throw the 2kg discus, while women must be under the age of 19 and throw the 1kg discus.)
There are, in addition, specifications for the diameters, thicknesses and tapers of the various discoi, and these can be found in the handbooks of the associations.

Aerodynamics of the Discus

The discus, in itself, is not an aerodynamic shape like the wing of an aircraft, but if it is tilted slightly in flight, it does experience a certain amount of aerodynamic lift, which adds to the distance it travels. We can't delve into the complex details of aerodynamics in this book, but suffice it

to say that best results are obtained when the initial path along which the discus travels as it leaves the hand makes an angle of about 35° to the horizontal, and when the plane of the discus has an angle with the horizontal slightly less than this, say 30°. For the right-handed thrower, a wind coming towards the circle along the right-hand sector line helps the aerodynamic lift considerably.

If your discus climbs rapidly in flight, then just drops almost vertically, it is an indication that you haven't got the correct angles as mentioned above.

The Technique

We will describe first the orthodox technique and later mention the variations that can be seen in the throwing of some top athletes.

The start

The thrower stands at the back of the circle, toes almost touching the rim, with the back turned to the direction of the throw. The feet are about shoulder-width apart, and the discus is held in the right hand with just the first phalanges of the comfortably spread fingers curling around the edge. The preliminary swings should be easy and relaxed, and for this reason we recommend that only one swing is taken to keep the skill simple. The hand should be above the discus during the swing and the turn — it will not drop out of the hand once the correct rhythm is mastered, since centrifugal force, due to rotation, will keep the discus in the hand. A slight tipping of the hand at each end of the swing is sufficient to prevent the discus dropping, though this should be kept to a minimum if range of movement is not to be impaired. Most throwers just lightly support the discus with the left hand as it reaches the end of the swing on that side. The bodyweight should shift to the side on which the discus is, and all the while, the back should be straight and nearly vertical.

6. The discus grip

Moving into the turn

At the end of the last swing the discus should be carried as far to the right rear of the thrower as his shoulder flexibility allows, while the right arm is kept horizontal so that the discus is at shoulder height. The left arm can aid this winding up if it is allowed to wrap around the chest. Just as, or slightly before, the right arm reaches the end of its backward travel you should 'cue in' the start of the drive into the turn by pushing the body-weight over the left foot while at the same time starting a ball-of-the-foot rotation over the left foot. The knees should bend, and there is a feeling of sitting into the turn with the knees turned outwards. You can think of turning the left knee round to the front of the circle, or you can think of 'grinding' the ball of the left foot into the concrete. The right arm must stay relaxed, holding the discus high behind the body. The essential thing at this stage is that the

23

Athletics: Throwing

bodyweight should be well over to the left without any tendency to fall backwards into the centre of the circle.

The drive, or run, across the circle
The movement across the circle is a running rotation. When the right foot comes off the ground from the starting position, that leg should be bent and

moved quickly to the centre of the circle. There will be a moment before the right foot touches down in the centre of the circle, when both feet will be in the air, but as this is a time when no force can be applied, it should be as short as possible, and this means that there must not be any bobbing up and down, and the movement must be a run rather than a jump.

7. *Discus technique: the sequence is of Rosemary Payne, British record holder*

2

3

7

8

13

14

Athletics: Throwing

Although no force can be applied to accelerate the thrower when he is air-borne, this phase should be used to regain the wound-up position, which will have been partially lost in the move into the turn. This advancing of the rotation of the lower body, in front of the upper body and the discus, can be achieved only if the legs are kept fairly close together (that is, the right leg must not sweep wide), while the upper body is allowed to trail behind from a relaxed and flexible waist.

The landing in the middle of the circle should be with the bodyweight over a well-bent right knee. It is the right leg which must start and contribute such a lot to the final throwing action, and it is not able to do this if the bodyweight goes too early to the front of the circle.

The left foot must follow the right foot very quickly, and snap down slightly to the left of the front of the circle. The knee will be bent, though not as much as that of the right leg.

The throwing action
At the end of the drive across the circle, the thrower should be in a powerful throwing position with his bodyweight well over a bent right leg, the left leg at the front of the circle slightly to the left of the line of the throw and with his upper body reaching far around behind him to the discus. There must be no hesitation or gathering for the throw here. Immediately the left foot reaches the front of the circle (some throwers actually start to throw before the left foot is down), the right leg starts to drive the right hip forwards and upwards. The left leg straightens, so the net effect is that the whole of the right side of the body is driven around a rigid left side. There is an unwinding of the upper body, and the discus is swept around wide on a long relaxed arm. At the moment that the discus leaves the hand it will be about shoulder level, and the body will be at full stretch with the chest high. There is no dropping of the left shoulder, nor is there any backward movement of the hips.

The final action of the wrist and fingers is one which gives the discus a clockwise (when seen from above) spin to stabilise it in flight. The attitude of the discus can be controlled by pressing down with the thumb in these final stages, and the discus should come off the index finger last.

The follow-through and recovery
In order to ensure a fluent throw without jerkiness, or slowing down in the delivery, it is essential that the right arm and shoulder be allowed to follow through and reach out after the discus. This, how-ever, must not carry you out of the front of the circle. The method used by most top throwers which permits a good follow-through without the possibility of a no-throw is called the 'reverse', and this is simply a reversal of the feet from the positions they are in as the delivery is made — the right foot comes forward, while the left is driven hard backwards. The driving of the left foot backwards causes a force tending to act against the general movement to the front of the circle, and if you drop your bodyweight slightly this will also help to prevent you toppling out the front. Some experienced throwers with particularly good balance continue the rotating action of the body, and perform another turn after the delivery, to allow a good follow-through.

Rhythm

Although we have split the throw up into sections, remember that the whole must be a continuous movement without any hesitations. Even top-class throwers do not accelerate the discus uniformly across the circle, but research has shown that their build-up of speed has less variation than that of novice throwers, so this smooth increase, from a fairly slow controlled start, to a flat-out delivery is obviously something to be worked for in training. A rushed start usually ends up in an inferior throw, though ideally, for very long throws, a really fast delivery is going to have to be tacked onto a fastish start.

Some Variations in Technique

If you watch the world's best throwers at an Olympics, you will see all kinds of idiosyncrasies and slight variations of the basic technique described above. The greatest variety is to be seen in the swing, or swings, where athletes get into some pretty wild contortions. We won't go into any of these, for we are convinced that simple swinging is the most effective. In the move into the turn, Jay Silvester, U.S.A., introduced the kicking action with the right leg, where the straight leg is swung forwards and to the left (of the thrower), instead of being bent and kept close to the body, as in the running across the circle method. This makes for an easy starting rhythm, and it also helps to get a good wind-up between the lower and upper body. The main disadvantage is that it may slow down your movement across the circle.

Faina Melnik, the women's world-record holder, uses a hammer-style heel and ball-of-the-foot turn on the left foot in the move into the turn. This allows a very fast turn, but it is a difficult skill to learn with all kinds of problems of balance.

In the delivery, there are two main schools of thought about the question of ground contact. The East Germans' technique calls for a firm planting of both feet during, and sometimes even after, delivery. This permits a good hip action, and is consistent in results. The disadvantages are that the follow-through is inhibited, and back soreness can result from the violent action of the hips. The Americans, on the other hand, tend to drive so hard with the back leg that it lifts them off the ground for the later stages of the delivery. The advantages are in speed and follow-through, but timing is more difficult and results are erratic.

John Powell, the men's ex-world-record holder, says that he thinks of the body movements in discus throwing being in the shape of an inverted 7. There is the movement sideways forming the top of the inverted 7, as the bodyweight goes over the left foot, then there is the down-stroke of the ⌐ in the drive across the circle in the direction of the throw.

There is a certain amount of contro-versy over the position of the left foot at the front of the circle. Old instructional books on discus throwing listed the so-called 'in-the-bucket' and 'blocking' movements of the left foot as bad faults to be eradicated at all costs. 'In-the-bucket' refers to the lazy left leg which stays in the air too long, and only comes down a long way to the left of the throwing line. The objection here is that the right leg then has very little to drive against and rotate around. This is a serious fault if it is combined with a too-early movement of the bodyweight across the circle from the starting position, for it means that almost no leg power goes into the throw. However, the fault can be compensated for if the rest of the technique is good and the right leg is able to be timed well in its drive, as was shown by Al Oerter, who had a tendency towards a late left leg at the time he won the 1968 Olympics. 'Blocking' refers to a premature grounding of the left foot at the front of the circle, which tends to prevent the right hip from coming through in the delivery. This is used deliberately by some throwers, such as the Olympic silver medallist Lothe Milde, to provide a solid base for powerful upper-body movements. It can be used when trying to remedy a thrower's fault of falling away to the left, but, as it can cause back injury, it is not to be recommended as correct technique.

Learning the discus throw
The full technique is a difficult one to learn and it is helpful for the beginner to try an easy progression from standing throws to walk-in throws to throws without swings.

Tips for Good Technique

1 Leave the discus trailing well behind the body throughout the throw by relaxing the upper body and moving the legs and hips fast.
2 The hand holding the discus should be kept up throughout the throw, since a low hand means a shorter radius and a slower moving discus.
3 Try to keep the shoulders level, and don't let the left shoulder drop away in the delivery.
4 Work for neat, fast footwork, think of 'twinkle-toes'!
5 Discus technique goes wrong at the back of the circle — make sure that you get your weight over your left foot before driving across the circle.
6 Continue to keep your bodyweight at the back of the circle for as long as possible, so that when you land in the middle ready for the delivery, the bodyweight is back over your right leg.
7 Snap the left leg down fast at the front of the circle, so that it lands slightly to the left of the line of the throw.
8 Relax and unwind into the release.

CHAPTER THREE

Javelin Throwing

History

Primitive man must have very early on discovered that a long pointed stick was an essential weapon for defending himself and also for hunting, so in this sense the javelin is the most basic of all the throwing events in athletics. Pictures on Ancient Greek pottery show men competing against each other in javelin throwing with techniques very similar to today's. But strangely enough, the event was late in coming to the Olympic Games, being contested for the first time at the 1908 London Games.

The Scandinavian countries have held a remarkable dominance of world javelin throwing from those early days right up to the present time. Matti Jarvinen of Finland was responsible for much technique development in the 1930s, and Scandinavians have taken many Olympic medals and produced more world-record breakers than all the other nations put together.

A major breakthrough in equipment was achieved by Bud and Dick Held of America, who first applied aerodynamic principles to javelin design. Bud Held went on to break the world record with one of these javelins, and this caused the authorities to introduce very strict and detailed specifications to limit the increasing distances being thrown. If they hadn't we might have witnessed a glider-type javelin flying outside the stadium by now!

The rules for the event were made 'cast-iron' about the time of the 1956 Olympics, when a club-level Spanish athlete discovered he could throw over the world record quite easily using a discus-type technique. Unfortunately for him, the method involved soaping the palm of the hand to facilitate the release, and this made the direction of flight highly unpredictable and dangerous for everyone inside the stadium, so the International Amateur Athletic Federation clamped down on the rules. Too bad for him, that he didn't keep his invention quiet until the Olympics! But he would have been fortunate indeed, if he had triumphed over Egil Danielsen's 85·71m/281ft 2in world record in those games. Since that time, the world record has come in for some really massive improvements by such greats as Terje Pedersen of Norway, Janis Lusis of the U.S.S.R., Jorma Kinnunen of Finland and Klaus

Athletics : Throwing

Wolfermann of West Germany.

The action of throwing a javelin, for anatomical reasons, seems to be an awkward one for women, and although they do have the advantage over men of extra shoulder mobility, this is not enough to compensate and their distances are much inferior. The weight of the javelin is not an important factor, and lowering the weight to 600gm, has not helped the ladies to get nearer the men's distances — in fact some top-class lady throwers think it would be an advantage to throw a heavier implement. Women's javelin did not enter the Olympic programme until 1932, when the famous Mildred 'Babe' Didrikson won at 43·70m/143ft 4in. The 1952 winner was Dana Zatopkova of Czechoslovakia, wife of the famous runner Zatopek.

The 1964 Games saw an interesting tussle, after Yelena Gorchakova of the U.S.S.R. set a world record of 62·38m/204ft 8in in the qualifying rounds, and then couldn't manage more than 57·06m/187ft 2in for third place in the final. Mihaila Penes of Rumania won there, but Gorchakova's world record stood for another eight years. Ruth Fuchs of East Germany won the 1972 Olympics with 63·88m/209ft 7in and she has been adding to the world record ever since, although her present 67·22m/220ft 6in is still a long way behind Klaus Wolfermann's men's record of 94·08m/308ft 8in.

Rules Affecting Technique

The rule, which effectively prescribes the technique to be used, runs as follows : 'The javelin must be held in one hand only, and at the grip, so that the little (or fourth) finger is nearest to the point. The javelin shall be thrown over the shoulder or upper part of the throwing arm, and must not be slung or hurled. At no time after preparing to throw, and until the javelin has been discharged, may the competitor turn completely round so that his back is towards the throwing arc. NON ORTHODOX STYLES ARE NOT PERMITTED.' (The capital letters are in the rule book!)

Specifications

Not only do the specifications for the javelin lay down the weight and length, but they also detail the size and weight of the metal head, the position of the centre of gravity, the position of the cord grip, the maximum diameter and the way in which the shaft should taper. Although these specifications seem pretty final as regards the type of javelin that may be used, they do allow some variations in design. Javelins are obtainable that vary in their attitude changes during flight. In some, the long-distance implements, the attitude changes very slowly, so that there is a delayed turning downwards of the point, whereas in others, the shorter-distance implements, the attitude changes much quicker, so that the point can come down sooner for an inexperienced thrower. As there is a rule which states : 'No throw shall be valid in which the tip of the metal head does not strike the ground before any other part of the javelin', it is essential that you choose the implement that best suits you.

You can find the detailed specifications for javelins in the handbooks of the athletic associations, but as you will need to know the particular javelin for your own age group we list the weights below :

Males

Age group	Age at 31st August/1st Sept.	Minimum weight of javelin
A.A.A. Men	19 and over	
A.A.A. Juniors	17 and 18	800gm/1lb 12·218oz
E.S.A.A. Seniors	17, 18 and 19	
A.A.A. Youths		
E.S.A.A. Intermediates	15 and 16	700gm/1lb 8·691oz
A.A.A. Boys		
E.S.A.A. Juniors	13 and 14	600gm/1lb 5·163oz

Females

W.A.A.A. and E.S.A.A.	All ages	600gm/1lb 5·163oz

Javelins are usually marked with their weights, so you should have no problem finding the appropriate implement for your group.
(Note that in international 'Junior' competition, men must be under the age of 20 in the year of the competition and throw the 800gm javelin, while women must be under the age of 19 and throw the 600gm javelin.)

The Technique

The grip
The main essential for consistent throwing is that there should be a full palm grip with the length of the javelin

8. Javelin grips: three ways of holding the javelin

binding lying along the length of the palm (not across the palm). It is harder to control the final attitude angle of the javelin if it rides up into just the fingers of the throwing hand. The grip should make use of the edge provided by the end of the binding, but there is no method of gripping this edge common to all top-class throwers. Some grip it with the thumb and first finger, some with the thumb and second finger and others with the first and second finger.

The approach run-up

The run-up has one purpose only, and that is to bring the body and the javelin into a powerful throwing position without any loss of the speed built up during the run. If you come to a stop before throwing you will have wasted the benefit of the run and you could just as well have performed a standing throw. There should be a gradual acceleration from the time you start to run, through the withdrawal phase, the cross-over strides and, of course, during the actual throw. In the withdrawal phase the javelin is dropped downwards and backwards, so that the throw can be made over as large a distance as possible. It is convenient to break the entire movement down into parts as follows, but remember that everything must flow smoothly without any breaks.

The preliminary run-up

This is the part of the approach run before the withdrawal phase, and, in an all-out throw, is usually about 12 strides. In training this can be reduced to as little as four or five strides. As the modern tendency is for faster and faster approach

runs, the javelin should be carried above the right shoulder with this arm as relaxed as possible, so as not to hinder the running action. Top-class throwers vary in the angle at which they carry the javelin, but a slightly point-up attitude is preferable.

The withdrawal phase

At the end of the preliminary run-up you should have a check mark on a spot which you will decide upon through a little practice. The withdrawal of the javelin, from over the shoulder to the rear and downwards, should then take place over the next two or three strides. We prefer just two as being simpler, but you will need three as your skill improves and you run faster, so you can take your choice, as long as you remember that with a two-stride withdrawal you must hit the checkmark with your left foot, and with a three-stride withdrawal you must hit it with your right. It is best to drop the javelin straight back, and not sideways, always keeping its length along the throwing line. Be careful not to tip the angle so that the tail hits the ground. The shoulders will need to start to turn sideways as the arm straightens, but don't let the hips turn — keep them going onwards as in the running action.

The cross stride

There is much controversy amongst coaches and throwers as to the best method of performing the cross stride. Some even avoid the use of the expression 'cross-over', preferring to call it, for example, an 'acceleration' stride. The purpose of this phase, anyway, is to prepare the body for the final throwing

9. Javelin technique : Hannu Siitonen, of Finland, winning the European Championship. The sequence starts immediately after the beginning of the withdrawal phase

2

3

5

6

8

9

10

11

12

13

14

15

16

17

18

stride, so it must place the thrower in a position in which his body is leaning backwards (while still moving forwards, of course!) with the throwing arm extended as far as possible to the rear. In order to prevent any slowing down, it is best if the hips are as square to the front as possible, with the feet trying to maintain a normal running stride. This means that the thrower must have both good hip and shoulder flexibility in order to reach backwards.

The throw

At the end of the cross stride the thrower's body will be in the leaning-backwards position with the bodyweight over the right heel, the throwing arm straight and the javelin in line with the direction of throw. Even before the front foot (left) touches the ground, the final delivery must begin without any hesitation or 'gathering', and the sequence of body movements is from the feet upwards. There will be a little sinking over the right leg as it lands, but then it must straighten, pushing the right hip forwards and the right heel outwards. The left arm aids the forward drive of the chest, and the head leans slightly to the left to allow the arm to whip through over the top of the body. The arm action is a true throwing action, with the elbow leading the implement. Remember that the arm pull must be along the length of the javelin. There will probably be a slight bending of the left knee as the full momentum of the body is absorbed, but then it should straighten, so that the final arm action is added to a straight left side.

The recovery

After the javelin has left the thrower's

hand the rest of his forward momentum has to be stopped as quickly as possible, so that he doesn't go over the scratch line, causing a no-throw. For this reason, he allows himself sufficient distance behind the line for the delivery, though obviously as little as he can spare, for the throw is measured from the scratch line. The best method of absorbing this forward speed is to 'reverse' the feet, the right leg coming through to the front, and then bending quickly as the bodyweight comes over it.

Tips for Javelin Throwing

1 Progress easily from slow controlled throws, and don't be in a hurry to perform flat-out run-ups.
2 Initially, in the learning stages, it may help if you talk to yourself as you reach the check mark: 'Check . . . one . . . two . . . three . . . cross . . . throw!'
3 Think of accelerating and stretching the legs out in front of you during the withdrawal and cross-over phases.
4 Continue the running action in the cross-over stride. Don't bring the right leg behind the left and don't shuffle.
5 Make sure that the right arm is straight before the arm strikes. Otherwise the action will be a short 'dart-throwing' one.
6 Keep the javelin straight along the line of the flight and pull along this line.
7 Remember that speed comes with relaxation.

CHAPTER FOUR

Hammer Throwing

History

Hammer throwing, as we know it today, has a short history, if we date it only from 1887, when the basic specifications for the implement and the throwing circle were drawn up. However, if we include sledge-hammers, shafted hammers and wheel hubs, then we can go back as far as 1800 BC, when at the Tailteann Games in Ireland the *'Roth Cleas'* or 'Wheel Feat' was contested. This may have involved the hurling of a complete chariot wheel, or perhaps a single spoke of a wheel plus hub. The event may have evolved from the ancient military sling, which was whirled round the head before the missile was projected. There is in existence a drawing of Henry VIII in the act of throwing a sledge-type hammer.

The *Encyclopaedia Britannica* credits the origin of the sport of hammer throwing to Ireland, where for centuries implements of various shapes and weights were thrown one-handed, two-handed, from the side, over the head, for distance, for height, from a run, from a stand, from an unlimited area and from a 9ft circle. The Scots are known to have used turning throws until 1860, when this was discontinued because of the danger to bystanders.

A special breed of men dominated modern style hammer throwing from the 1890s to the 1930s — they were the Irish Americans, known as the 'Irish Whales' because of their huge physiques. For example, there was the great all-rounder John Flanagan, who won the 1900, 1904 and 1908 Olympic hammer titles — only Al Oerter in the discus has surpassed this feat — and there was Pat Ryan, whose world record of 57·76m/189ft 6in lasted for 25 years.

The Germans emerged as hammer-throwers in the 1930s, and in the process they re-thought the technique. They rejected the jump turns of the men before them, and developed the modern heel and ball-of-foot turning action in which ground contact is maintained throughout the throw. In 1938 the German, Erwin Blask, set the world record at 59m/193ft 7in and there it stayed for another ten years.

The East Europeans took over the hammer-throwing scene after the war, with domination by first the Hungarians, then the Russians, who showed the athletics world a new technique — a lean-away and a progressively increasing lead on the hammer from start to delivery. The

American Hal Connolly gained the world record in 1956, and steadily improved it until it went back to the Hungarians again in 1965, when Gyula Zsivotsky startled the world with an amazing 73·74m/ 241ft 11in. But it hasn't stopped there — the Russians and the Germans have come back and, in turn, have steadily pushed the world record upwards in a manner which reminds one of money inflation! In 1975, for instance, five men threw beyond the record standing in 1974, with Walter Schmidt of West Germany getting in the final word at 79·30m/260ft 2in. Where will it end? Perhaps the International Amateur Athletic Federation will decide to alter the specifications to shorter and/or heavier hammers, since these ever-increasing distances are becoming a safety hazard.

Specifications
Weights are as follows:

Age group	Age at 31st August/1st Sept.	Minimum weight of hammer
A.A.A. Men	19 and over	7·257kg/16lb
A.A.A. Juniors E.S.A.A. Seniors	17 and 18 17, 18 and 19	6·25kg/13lb 8oz
A.A.A. Youths E.S.A.A. Intermediates	15 and 16	5kg/11lb
A.A.A Boys E.S.A.A. Juniors	13 and 14	4kg/8lb 13oz

(Note that in international 'Junior' competition, men must be under the age of 20 in the year of competition and throw the 7·257kg hammer.)

The rules also state a minimum length, measured from the inside of the grip to the farthest point of the head, but the critical measurement is really the maximum length, since an expert thrower will ensure that his hammer is as near to this as possible. The maximum length is 121·5cm/3ft 11·835in. There are other specifications, and these can be found in the handbooks of the associations. Your school, club or local sports dealer will be able to supply you with a hammer, but you should check regularly that its length and weight are correct.

Safety
Safety is particularly important in hammer throwing, since the implement travels so fast and is such a lethal weapon. You, as the thrower, are responsible to see that no one is in danger when you throw, and as the hammer can fly off in any direction, you should always throw from a circle

within a safety cage. Even so, don't let anyone stand close to the netting — it is not a brick wall — and make sure that anyone within the landing area, is alerted before you throw. There is no excuse for releasing a hammer into the cage when you have lost control of the throw, except in the extreme emergency situation. You should check your hammer before each throw to reduce the chances of it coming apart in mid-throw. Keep the wire straight, and don't allow the handle to strike the cage.

Rules Affecting Technique

The rules do not specify any particular technique and as long as you can satisfy the general rules of throwing — such as not touching, with the body, the ground outside the circle during the throw, and so on — you may use one hand or two hands, perform a standing throw, or turn as many times as you wish.

The Technique

Although the rules don't limit the technique, as they do in the shot and javelin, the modern technique has become fairly well stereotyped to two swings and three turns before delivery. A few top-class throwers use three swings, and some perform four turns. Two swings are sufficient to get the implement moving, and the size of the circle limits most people to three turns. Only very neat turning, or a special technique in the first turn allows the possibility of four turns. However, it is going to be some time before you even get beyond a single turn, never mind three!

Before thinking about how the beginner should actually go out and throw the hammer the first few times, let us first describe a good simple throwing technique. In essence, a thrower swings the hammer round his head twice, turns three times and throws it away over his left shoulder. In slightly more detail, a hammer thrower swings the hammer twice around his head, while his feet remain almost stationary at the rear of the circle and pointing in the opposite direction to that of the throw. At the end of the second swing the thrower initiates a whole body turning action with his feet, rotating with his weight over his left foot. The gradually accelerated rotation carries him to within several centimetres of the front of the circle after three turns, and he uses the third turn to give the hammer a final large delivery acceleration, releasing it high, around and over the left shoulder. The plane of the path of the hammer throughout is inclined at an angle, so that the release angle is near 45°. The plane is also turned to the thrower's right side.

Starting position
There are several methods of starting the swings, but here is one simple efficient way. The gloved left hand is placed in the handle, so that the grip rests along the middle phalanges of the fingers, and the right-hand fingers are placed over the left. Stand at the rear of the circle with the toes almost touching the rim, so that your back is towards the direction of the throw. Your feet should be comfortably spaced about shoulder-width apart. Swing the hammer head backwards and to the right, twisting the body with the implement. Drop the hammer head on to the ground as far back

10. Hammer grip and starting position. Andrew demonstrates a simple starting position. The inset shows the grip for a right-handed thrower

the bodyweight to the left. The arms should sweep the hammer in a wide path, remaining straight until they reach the high point above and in front of the left shoulder. As the hands pass over your head, twist the trunk back to the right rear to meet the hammer, shifting the bodyweight on to the right foot. The hammer head falls with its low point a little ahead of its original position at the start, clearing the ground by 5–10cm. The second swing is carried out similarly to the first, though slightly faster. The arms are kept long and relaxed – think of them as an extension of the hammer wire, and do not attempt to influence the movement of the hammer through any arm or shoulder muscle action. The usual fault seen in a beginner's swing is the tendency to flex the arms and pull the hammer inwards. This upsets the rhythm and results in jerkiness. Once the hammer has been lifted from the ground, at the start, the effort must come from the lower body only, the arms and shoulders remaining passive.

The transition

The transition is the link between the swings and the turns. Continue the second swing, sweeping the hammer out on long relaxed arms, as the bodyweight shifts back on to the left leg. Be careful not to cut the second swing short by a sudden movement of the upper body turning to the left. Think of starting to turn the left foot as the hammer head reaches the low point. This should ensure that your body leads the hammer up to the high point, but that excessive lead does not develop at this stage to cause a shortening of the radius.

as is comfortable without moving the feet, weight on the right foot, and arms as straight as possible. This is the elementary starting position.

The swings

Lift the hammer with the arms and trunk, so that the hammer head goes forwards (relative to your body) and upwards. As the hammer head comes to the front, shift

11. Hamm
technique
Valentin Dmitrenk
U.S.S.R., who hol
the British A
Comers' reco
exhibitir
remarkable contr
in an orthodox tw
swing, three-tu
thro

Athletics: Throwing

Footwork in the turns

The filmed sequences of Dmitrenko show the footwork in the turns. Note that bodyweight is kept mainly over the left foot throughout the three turns, and that the left foot does most of the work, with only a little help from the right. The first part of the turn, through some 180°, is on the heel of the left foot (while the right foot remains in contact with the ground most of the time, assisting in the turning action) and then the second 180° is turned on the outside edge of the ball of the left foot. The beginner's turns are not automatic, so you must practise them until you can be precise in your movements, ensuring that each rotation is through 360°. Under- or over-turning can cause problems, in that the edge of the circle is reached before three turns are completed. The right leg should not thrash about — the thighs should be kept close together, since a wide sweep of the right leg slows the rotation of the body and allows the hammer to overtake the thrower.

Body action in the turns

The knees are bent, and the shoulders and arms must remain relaxed throughout the turns, while the movement is made with the feet and lower body. With the arms relaxed and the correct timing of the lower-body action, you will feel a 'contact' force or tension up the left arm to the shoulder. Maintain this 'contact' all the way through the throw, but remember that the tension in the arm must come from the hammer's centrifugal pull, which in turn comes from the lower-body action — there must be no muscular force in the arms.

It is difficult to turn efficiently on straight legs, so keep the legs flexed at the knees. This knee flexion is necessary for the lift at delivery anyway.

The hips play an important part in the throw, and by twisting at the waist, the lower body can be made to lead the hammer head. The amount of lower-body lead varies during the turns, with very little as the hammer travels up from the low point to the high point, but the lead increases during the one-foot-contact phase, with maximum occurring as the right foot touches down again. The amount of the lead increases from turn to turn until, at the end of the third turn, the body is really well wound up for the delivery. All the while, keep your head in as natural a position as possible, with no hunching of the shoulders.

Balance

Correct balance is, perhaps, the most important single factor in the hammer throw, since without it rhythm is lost and the throw has to be 'muscled' out. The correct amount of body lean to counter-balance the pull of the hammer will be with the bodyweight well over the left foot, so that you don't fall heavily on to the right foot at the end of each turn.

The rhythm

The third turn should be at maximum speed — not the first! Start slowly and build up the speed of the hammer head gradually, from swing to swing and turn to turn.

The delivery

Think of *lift*. Try to straighten the body until it is on tip-toe in one great explosive lift, as the hammer is accelerated by the last rapid unwinding of the body.

Recovery

If the turns have been carried out with precise and neat footwork, the thrower should complete his delivery with room to spare to the circle rim, and, if balance has been good, there should be no falling about once the hammer has been released.

Learning to Throw the Hammer

The beginning of learning to throw the hammer is a most difficult stage, because the movements involved are so unlike any others in the whole of sport. Perhaps this is one reason why hammer throwing is a minority event — the beginner immediately becomes aware of the vast difference between his own efforts and those of even a mediocre thrower, and he assumes that the technique is too much for him. But herein lies the enjoyment to be had from learning the hammer — you can improve until the day you retire!

Fortunately, the nature of hammer throwing is well suited to the part-progression method of learning, in which you can release the hammer at any of a number of intermediate stages. For example, the hammer can be thrown progressively after one or two swings, after one turn, two turns or three turns. In order not to develop faults, it is best to get on to the full three turns as soon as your skill permits. Practices involving turning without releasing may not be so exciting, but they are a great help in learning the technique. Learning the hammer does require more expert advice than the other events in athletics, and it is essential that you obtain help from a coach in the early stages.

Tips for Good Hammer Throwing

1 Relax the arms and shoulders, so that you feel 'contact' with the hammer.
2 Maintain balance over the left side in the turns.
3 Settle for nothing less than perfect and automatic footwork.
4 Start slowly, accelerate smoothly and finish fast.
5 Build up a lead by working the hips, especially from the high point.
6 Lift in the delivery.

CHAPTER FIVE

Training

How Often?

The international-standard thrower, aiming to represent his country at an Olympics, will be training very hard twice a day almost every day. He will not have much time for other things if he is working or studying, and this is the kind of dedication that is required to reach the top. But we don't expect that many of the readers of this book will want to sacrifice so many of the interests in a varied life, so we must look at the kind of training necessary to become a good club, or school, athlete. Skill-learning research has shown that ability increases most rapidly when the skill is practised once every 24 hours. Little and often is better than a lot infrequently, so ideally you will need to train at throwing for a short while each day. However, you also need to gain strength and mobility. Weight training is the best method of gaining and maintaining strength, but here again you will need to lift weights on up to four days per week. You can train for mobility by doing stretching exercises during each day's warm-up, so this is not such a problem. The question is one of effecting a compromise between skill and strength training. We recommend something like the

following as a minimum for the person whose main sport is a throwing event:

Monday: weights
Tuesday: throw
Wednesday: weights
Thursday: throw
Friday: rest
Saturday: competition (weights and throw if no competition)
Sunday: throw

Each session should last one hour, of which ten minutes is a warm-up.

Provided that you don't waste time getting changed, and provided that you don't have to travel far for your training facilities, you will find that the total of about an hour and a half is well spent, and the stimulation of the exercise will actually help you to work and study better.

Throwing Training

Quality
The thrower who bashes out hundreds of throws at maximum effort is unlikely to progress very far, and he will probably

give up the event in frustration after a few months. The throwers with that vital edge are those who think about what they are doing, and know what they are trying to achieve – and preferably have a coach watching during most sessions.

Although a skill should not be practised at a vastly different speed to that normally required, it is unlikely that new techniques can be tried when throwing at all-out speed. Continual throwing at maximum effort is certain to consolidate bad habits and wrong technique. Don't carry that measuring tape to training sessions! In training, the uppermost thought in the thrower's mind must be some point of technique – for example, a discus thrower may think: 'In the next throw I am going to concentrate on the correct move-ment of my bodyweight over the left foot at the rear of the circle.' He will have several throws with this as the main point of concentration, before going on to a different aspect.

Quantity
Don't aim to complete a set number of throws per session – stop when you feel pleasantly tired, or when the skill is getting shaky. Remember that a dozen throws performed well and correctly thought out are better than 50 slovenly, mindless attempts.

Circle discipline
When you throw from a circle, be strict with yourself about staying in the circle during and after delivery. Bad habits learned in training in this connection are certain to carry over into competition – or worse still, the technique in competition, which requires you to stay within the circle, will be vastly different from the technique of using the extra distance when stepping out of the circle during training.

How many implements?
To save time in recovering the implement you have thrown, it is a good idea to have more than one to train with, if they are available. It usually is a matter of preference, and, although most discus-throwers like to use two or three discoi, hammer-throwers generally prefer just one hammer.

Heavy implements
Some strength training and a lot of technique training can be achieved through the use of implements heavier than the normal for your particular age group. It is wise not to go too far above the specified weight, so that the technique you use is not altered too much. For instance a girl discus-thrower will benefit from having five or six throws with a 1·25kg discus at some of her throwing sessions. In the case of the hammer, one can also shorten the length of the wire, as well as increasing the weight, and in this way the weight can be even doubled, without affecting the technique a great deal. Javelin throwers use small weighted balls or lumps of metal to simulate an increased weight of javelin, and these are particularly helpful when you are concen-trating on some aspects of technique.

Light implements
We can't do much to improve the speed of contraction of individual muscles, but it is possible to improve the speed of a throw by training to help the co-ordination of the movement. General improvement in a thrower's skill will almost automatically

Athletics: Throwing

lead to greater speed, but progress can sometimes be helped by using lightweight implements. However, as with heavy implements, you should go only a little down in weight and restrict the amount of this type of training.

You can accustom yourself to faster muscle movements by means of sprint running. Introduce 'wind' sprints into the later part of your warm-up before a training session. Run about 50m with speed being increased up to the halfway mark, then run flat-out for the rest of the way.

Warming-up

Before any kind of training, throwing or weight training, you should prepare your body gradually for the severe exercise you are about to undertake by warming-up. The scientific basis for the warm-up is still not clear, but it does increase the blood flow to the musculature, decreases the muscle viscosity and raises the body temperature slightly. It also has a psychological effect, for, in performing a throwing skill at a low level of effort, the neuro-muscular system is 'reminded' and prepared for the exercise to follow. For these reasons, a gentle warm-up lasting about ten minutes will reduce the risk of injuries. You will no doubt develop your own favourite warm-up routine, but to

get you started try the following:

Jog about 800m ($\frac{1}{2}$ mile).

Do three or four minutes of stretching exercises of the Yoga type.

Throw several times at about half effort with a single implement, and run hard to collect it each time.

Before a weights session you can omit the last part and substitute a set or two of power snatches with light weights (see later).

It is also a good idea to include a warm-down jog at the end of each session, for this will reduce any tendency for the muscles to stiffen up.

Strength Training

Assistance exercises to increase strength are a must for any thrower wishing to achieve respectable distances. Weight training is the tried and trusted strength-gaining method of the world's top athletes, and you will be surprised at how effective it can be if used sensibly. Results will begin to show after a few months, and although there will be periods of apparent non-improvement, you will continue to grow stronger as long as you train at weights. If you haven't ever lifted any weights, or even if you have, but have had a break for a few months, the following schedule is a good one (see the illustrations also) to start on:

High pull (or power snatch)	12$\frac{1}{2}$kg/25lb	× 10 repetitions	× 2 sets
Curl	,,	,,	,,
Press behind neck	,,	,,	,,
Squat	25kg/50lb	,,	,,
Bench Press	,,	,,	,,
Abdominal sit-ups	no weight	,,	,,

12

13

12. Weight training: Christine and Gillian show the starting and finishing positions of the exercise. In the High Pull the weight is lifted from the floor to arm's length above the head in one smooth movement, which keeps the bar close to the body throughout

13. The Curl: a reverse grip is used to bring the bar to the neck without too much whole-body sway

14. The Press Behind Neck: good for upper-body strength and mobility

15. The Squat: the best exercise there is for leg strength — so lift with the legs!

14

15

16 The Bench Press: use a wide grip on the bar bell

17. Abdominal Sit-up: helps to keep the waist trim as well as being an excellent conditioning exercise for all throwers

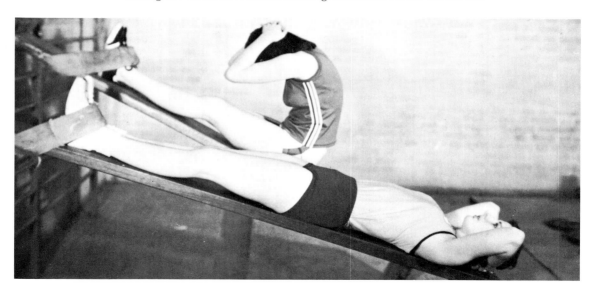

This schedule requires only about 20 minutes to complete, even with a minute's rest in between sets, and preferably should be done twice or three times per week. You should increase the weights by 2½kg/5lb every week (the high pull doubles as a warm-up exercise, so it should not be done with more than about 25kg/50lb until you are more experienced). When you have carried out this schedule faithfully for two months you will be ready for a new one, and you should seek help from a coach, or experienced athlete. Because you become accustomed to handling weights, you will be capable of increasing the poundages, and reducing the number of repetitions in each set. Many throwers, seeking to increase strength, are of the opinion that repetitions in a set never need

50

to be more than five or six (except in the high pull used as a warm-up, and the abdominal sit-ups, where no weight is used anyway). Some train with the so-called pyramid system, in which they start the particular exercise with a weight they can just manage to lift five times. After a rest, the weight is increased a little and four repetitions are performed. This process is repeated until two repetitions are pushed up with the heaviest weight that can be managed. Once every few weeks a personal best is attempted on a single repetition, and if it is successful, the starting weight for the set of five repetitions is increased at the next session.

From time to time you will need to introduce new exercises into your weights schedule, and you should work out (preferably with a coach's help) some specific exercises to assist your particular throwing event. For instance, a discus-thrower will try the discus action with a dumb-bell in each hand while lying on an inclined bench (the 'flying exercise'), and a shot-putter may do a front press with the bar going up explosively at 45° (the 'Nieder press').

Weight training for girls
A special word to the ladies here: in spite of myths and fallacies to the contrary, which you may have heard, gentle weight training never made anybody muscle-bound. You need special exercises, special diets and extremely strenuous training before you begin to look like a Mr Universe. The argument which points to the huge sizes of some of the world's top women throwers is not a very good one — they were big *before* they started training. Big girls tend to be attracted to

the throws, it is not the training which makes them big. The kind of training recommended here, will serve only to increase your strength, firm your body a little, and make you look and feel a lot better.

Safety
Weights can be dangerous, if used incorrectly, so observe the following safety rules if you wish to stay free of injuries:

1 Always lift a weight from the ground with the heels down flat, keep the back straight and keep the trunk nearly vertical, as you lift with the legs. You may cause injury to your spine if you try to lift a heavy weight with your back only.
2 Always wear shoes when training (that is, don't lift weights in bare feet).
3 Put your weights in the racks, or places provided, when you have finished an exercise, and don't leave the floor cluttered. You, or someone else, may trip over weights left lying about.
4 Take care that no one else is in danger when you lift a weight, and make sure that no one is lifting weights overhead nearby, if you are doing an exercise which involves lying down.
5 Keep your squatting exercise within reasonable poundages, since your knee joints and lower spine are vulnerable areas in this movement. It is a most valuable exercise, nevertheless, if performed sensibly.
6 Work well within your capacity, and try to lift personal bests only on the rare occasion. When you do try a very heavy lift, have a helper at each end

of the bar ready to catch the weight if you are in trouble.

7   Don't indulge in horseplay in the weights gymnasium.

Jumping Exercises

A thrower needs plenty of explosive strength in the legs, and, in addition to weight training, it is a good idea to incorporate jumping exercises in the programme. Standing and running long jumps, standing and running triple jumps, five double-footed bounds and combinations of hops, steps and jumps (such as hop, hop, step, step, jump) all go to help make leg-strength training enjoyable. Try also to see how few hops on one foot it takes you to cover 50m, then try on the other foot. Place five or six low hurdles about 1m apart and see if you can manage double foot hops over them without stopping. Ordinary high jumping is a useful exercise, but also try diving over the bar from a two-footed take-off.

Mobility

Body mobility is much neglected by throwers. The vital hip and shoulder areas should be loosened up every day in the warming-up process. We have found that a gentle jog, followed by Yoga exercises, are best for helping mobility. Always relax slowly into the fully stretched position of a joint — don't use ballistic, bouncing movements, since these are self-defeating and can cause injury.

Endurance

A thrower requires a certain amount of endurance to maintain top form throughout a competition, which may last up to $1\frac{1}{2}$ hours if there are many competitors. Run around the track or field a few times at the beginning of each training session. Circuit training once or twice a week during winter will ensure that you are fit for a lot of throwing when the spring comes. (Circuit training consists of about a dozen exercises, e.g. step-ups on a bench, press-ups on the floor, vertical jumps, etc., which are performed one after the other without a rest in between.) Swimming about 500m two or three times a week is excellent for endurance and relaxation, as are many indoor games such as badminton, squash and basketball.

Diary

Get into the habit of keeping a diary of your training. You will find that you can develop a short-hand method, and, with just one or two comments about the way you felt during the session, it shouldn't take you more than a few minutes to write up each night. The way you have trained, and the results you have achieved will be valuable information when you come to plan your schedules the following year.

Rest

You should have a rest from training one day per week, and once a month you should rest completely for three or four days. Give your body time to recover and build up nervous energy by resting the day before a competition. For the really big competitions about twice a year, try a two-day lay-off beforehand.

CHAPTER SIX

Competition

Preparation

How you act and think in the 48 hours before a competition, and during the competition, can have a considerable influence on the distance you achieve. What may be good for one thrower may not be good for you, but most agree that adequate rest is vital.

Mental preparation is very important, so that you are ready at the start of the competition with just the correct amount of nervous energy and determination for the long throws. If you are naturally a worrier, and your nerves reduce you to a weak mass at the start of each competition, then your mental preparation should aim at forgetting about the competition in the hours previous to it. The best way to arrive at this state is to compete as often as you can until you become so conditioned to the prospect of competition that it no longer upsets you. If you are the lazy, easy-going type, you may have to use a different approach — you may have to induce a state of nervousness by thinking constantly about the competition. There are some athletes who can work themselves into a mood of fierce determination, so that they produce performances way above their usual — the more important the competition, the greater is their drive.

Allow yourself plenty of time to travel to the venue of the competition, and make sure that you have packed your bag with all you will require. At the ground, ensure that everything is in order with your entry, report to the stewards, and obtain your numbers — all in good time.

Start your warm-up at the moment which will allow you to reach your peak physical, technical and mental condition for the first throw. Be flexible and prepared to adjust, or stop, the warm-up, if there are delays.

Competition Strategy

If there is a large number of competitors, you may have to wait a long while between throws, and, as this will be entirely different from the conditions under which you have trained, you should know how to cope with the situation. It is important that your very first throw should be a good one — both in the sense of being valid, and in terms of distance achieved. There is nothing more nerve-racking than to have a no-throw at the first attempt,

Athletics: Throwing

and have to wait 20 minutes for the second. On the other hand, there is nothing more likely to unnerve your opponents than a 'scorcher' from you in the first round.

During the competition, keep your concentration going. Don't talk unless absolutely necessary, keep away from the circle between throws and work up mental energy for the next throw. Every competition throw is a chance to produce a personal best. Remember that the competition is neither won nor lost until the end of the final round. If your distance is bettered by a rival, don't give up — rather let it be an incentive for you to relax, go even faster and drive even harder in the delivery in your next throw. This is the real thrill of good competition: to have your rivals' good performances draw you out beyond what you thought you could do. You can watch them taking their turns to throw, especially when they are more advanced technically than you, for you will learn from them, but don't become so concerned with what is going on in that circle that you lose your own concentration.

Competition Behaviour

To me, athletics is about people, and how you relate to them, as you strive to get the best performance from yourself. As in all sports, there are unwritten rules of behaviour in the throwing events. Many of these have to do with the safety of people around you, so when you are about to throw make sure they are all aware of it. Don't jump your turn in the queue by the circle when warming-up; don't walk in the field of view of the athlete about to throw; and don't chatter when someone is throwing. Be courteous to officials at all times, and remember to thank them at the end of a competition — they are giving up their time for you.

Remain modest and quiet even when you do win and throw a long way, for the athlete who brags is a bore. Your results will speak for you.

Never lose your temper because you are throwing badly. Win or lose, keep in mind that it is only a game, and, in the words of Baron de Coubertin, the taking part is the most important thing.

CHAPTER SEVEN

Throwing Events in Scottish Highland Games

The so-called 'heavy events' for men in Scottish Highland Games consist of throwing the Scots hammer, putting the shot, putting the stone, throwing the 28-lb hammer, tossing the caber, throwing the 56lb weight over the bar for height and tossing the sheaf. As you can well imagine, a great deal of fun can be had at these events, especially as the Scots officials will probably give you an added handicap by insisting that you wear a kilt. The heavy events are contested wherever there is a Scottish Highland Games, and, as the Scots have emigrated to the four corners of the globe, and taken their customs with them, you need not be surprised if there are cabers and hammers flying once a year in the park at Mufulira, Zambia!

There are both professional and amateur Highland Games, so if you wish to retain your amateur status, you should not enter a professional one. However, the amateur games, especially those run in Scotland, often offer handsome prizes and attract 'pot hunters' from far afield. You will find many Games advertised, with entry details, in the magazine *Athletics Weekly*, obtainable at most bookshops.

The Scots Hammer

This is a 16-lb ball on the end of a 4ft wooden shaft and the rules for throwing it are very restrictive: they forbid the use of whole body turns, and you are allowed to swing the implement around your head only with your feet stationary. The rules call for a rectangular wooden stopboard to be fixed to the ground, and it is from behind this that the throw is made. Stepping over the board, or the line through it, counts as a no-throw. The throw is made from grass, and you are allowed to dig holes for your feet, which you may fix even more securely by fitting long horizontal spikes or knives into the toes of your boots. An expert thrower digs his feet into holes about $\frac{1}{2}$m behind the wooden stopboard, so that his back is to the direction of the throw. He grasps the hammer shaft with the left hand at the top and the right hand immediately below it. Starting with the hammer head on the ground forward and to the right of his right foot, he swings the implement round his head three or four times before delivering it over his left shoulder. Movement of the feet in a follow-through is allowed. This all sounds very much like a standing throw with the wire hammer,

18. *The Scots Hammer: British record holder Alex Valentine about to deliver the 17·25kg/16lb ball on a shaft*

parks or fields devoid of concrete circles, and the thrower has to come to terms with slippery, sloping grass surfaces. The 'stone' will be thrown from the same circle, though local rules may allow only a standing throw. Usually the stone is enormous, weighs about 10 to 15kg (20 to 30lb), is only vaguely spherical, and presents a real problem when you try to put it it with one hand. However the local Scots will be fiercely proud of their stone, and will put up a valuable prize and trophy for the winner, so it is well worth entering the event!

Throwing the 28-lb Hammer
The 28-lb hammer is a huge ball of iron fixed to a short length of chain (40cm/16in overall) with a triangular handle and has to be thrown from a 2·5m/8ft 2½in diameter circle. The experienced thrower of a wire hammer comes into his own here, for his technique is superior to

19. *The 12·5kg/28lb hammer testing the limits of Howard Payne's strength*

but the sensation is quite different — the plane of movement of the hammer head is turned more to the front of the thrower, and there is a pronounced lean back of the upper body in order to flatten the plane. The centrifugal forces built up in the swings are quite high, and to help prevent the hammer slipping out of his grip, the thrower usually puts liquid resin on his hands and on the shaft.

Putting the Shot and the Stone
The shot used at Highland Games is exactly the same as that used in normal athletics, though many venues are in

that used by the Scots-style throwers. If you have thrown the wire hammer you will only have to modify your technique by eliminating one swing. The circle is so big you can even manage four turns, if you wish. The only snag is that you will probably be throwing off a grass circle, and you will be lucky indeed if the surface is level!

The Scots-style technique is a one-handed affair, very similar to throwing the discus, except that $2\frac{1}{2}$ turns are used. The extra turn is relatively easy to fit in, because the enormous weight ensures that the first turn is rather slow. You have to be very strong to achieve any worthwhile distance with this method.

Tossing the Caber

The caber is part of a tree trunk, and there are no specifications laid down to standardise the event from competition to competition. It can vary in length up to a maximum of about 5m/16ft, and the weight can reach about 90kg/200lb or so, which means that you need to be rather strong even to lift it off the ground! Helpers carry the caber over to the starting area, where they stand it up on its thinner end. The thrower takes hold while the helpers beat a hasty retreat to a safe distance. He bends down with his right shoulder against the lower end of the caber, puts his arms around it and joins his hands together with fingers interlaced. He has now to give a sharp lift upwards and, as soon as the caber comes off the ground, has to quickly bring his hands, with fingers still interlaced, under the end which was on the ground. He stands up, using his hands and shoulder

to balance the top-heavy pole. The whole caber must be inched upwards until the hands are at chest level, elbows pointing outwards. The thrower then has to tip the caber slightly forward, and start a run of about 30m. He stops abruptly and this causes the caber to tilt forwards, to which he adds extra momentum by a well-timed lift with the arms. The caber should land on its thick end and continue rotating over, so that the thin end lands farthest away from the thrower. The judges look at the throw in terms of the numbers on a clock face — the thrower is at 6 o'clock, the thick end comes down at the centre of the dial, and the final position of the thin end must point towards any part of the clock between 9 and 3, the winner being the one whose toss gets nearest to 12

20. Caber technique: Bill Fuller, one of Britain's best all-round throwers, makes a perfect 12 o'clock toss ▶

2

3

4

5

6

7

8

9

10

o'clock. If the caber's thin end drops backwards into the semicircle between 3 and 9 o'clock, the attempt is considered a no-toss.

The choice of the caber to be used, and rules concerning number of attempts, and whether progressively lighter cabers are brought into the competition, or whether the one caber is shortened gradually by sawing pieces off it, until one competitor succeeds in tossing it, depend upon the local organisation of that particular competition. Just one thing is certain — you, the thrower, and everyone around will have great fun! A word of caution though — the caber is a heavy, potentially dangerous object. If it should start to topple before you are ready to toss it, just let it go and get out of the way. If you try to wrestle with it you may injure yourself.

Throwing the 56-lb Weight for Height

This event makes use of the type of 56-lb weight which has a ring support at the top, and it is this ring which the thrower holds during the throw. The cross-bar is supported on pole-vault stands, which are capable of raising the bar to some 5m/ 16ft, though competitions usually start at around 3m/10ft. The event is run exactly like a high-jump or pole-vault competi-

21. The 15kg/56lb weight: Britain's all-time great, Arthur Rowe, heaves the 56-lb weight over the bar.

tion, except that the purpose is to throw the 56-lb weight over the bar without dislodging it. A competitor is knocked out of the competition on his third successive failure, and ties are resolved on fewest failures, etc., as in the jumps.

Athletics: Throwing

There are several different ways of throwing this weight — with one hand, with two hands, body sideways on to, or with the back towards, the cross-bar. All involve a preliminary swing of the weight, in a vertical plane, which brings it between the legs for the start of the final upswing. Arms and shoulders should be as long and relaxed as possible, and all the work should be done with the legs and back. A well-timed swing and lift should end with the body fully extended in a follow-through upwards towards the crossbar.

Finally, another note of caution — the 56-lb weight *is* heavy, and can cause injury, if not thrown properly, so don't attempt it unless you are at least stronger than the average 16 year old.

Tossing the Sheaf
You will find this event only at some of the more traditional Games in rural areas. It has obviously developed from the pitchforking of hay in farming, and involves picking a heavy bundle, or bag, of hay up with a pitchfork, and tossing it over a bar for height. The best technique is to hold the end of the pitchfork in the right hand, and have the left well down the shaft near the fork end. Place your body between the sheaf and the cross-bar. The fork should be stuck into the sheaf with the curved side away from you (i.e. the concave side should be away from you). The throw now consists of a powerful lift with the left hand, until it is above the right, then a lifting with both arms until the fork is vertical and high above the head. A quick jerk gives the sheaf a little extra momentum, and also frees the fork, sending the sheaf sailing over the bar — you hope!

CHAPTER EIGHT

Throwing the Wellington Boot

Wellie wanging, or throwing the gumboot, is a fairly recent innovation, and although it may seem a frivolous pastime it is taken seriously by some throwers, perhaps because organisers are inclined to put up valuable prizes for the winners. The rules, and the boot's air resistance, make it a most frustrating event, and the winner is not always the best thrower, but rather the one who manages to catch the wind

22. Gumboot throwing: TV personality George Roper demonstrating abysmal Wellie-wanging technique! International sprinter, Brian Green, who is an expert boot-thrower, is to the left of George, and Howard Payne, world record holder at this event, is standing on the platform (Photo by courtesy of Dunlop Ltd.)

just right, while, at the same time, flighting the Wellie straight down the middle of the landing area.

The rules state that the boot must be a regulation size 8 boot, weigh approximately 1kg/35oz and measure about 40cm/16in long. The field must be level, the boot must remain within an 'alley' 10m (32ft 10in) wide, and the distance must be measured from a clearly defined throwing line.

The greatest release speed of the boot can be obtained using a modified discus technique, in which the boot is held at the top, in one hand. The angle of release should be a lot lower than in the discus, but a good spin, as in discus-throwing, is necessary. The best flight is usually obtained if the toe of the boot leads. Unfortunately, with a discus turn it is difficult to flight the boot down the area bounded by the parallel lines only 10m apart, and some people resort to overarm-bowling methods, sacrificing distance for accuracy.

The one advantage that Wellie wanging has over the other throwing events is that you don't have to worry about the safety of spectators, for an errant boot is fairly soft and unable to do much damage!

CHAPTER NINE

Conclusion

The throwing events in athletics have a great deal to offer you. If you can't hold your own with the runners and the jumpers, you can try the throws, where you will find that sheer physical ability, though an advantage, is not enough for success. If you are intelligent and determined, you will soon be out-throwing people who are more 'athletic' than yourself. You will gain friends from amongst your fellow athletes and officials, and the travel involved will open up a whole world of new horizons. The exercise can only be beneficial to your health and well-being, and is a useful way of giving vent to any emotional stresses of our present-day, high-pressure living. You will discover yourself through coping with the successes and failures you will experience in competition, and in all probability these will help to make you a better person to know.

Good throwing!